The Timeless Martini

Evolution of the Iconic Cocktail, with a Century of Recipes and Lore

by Michael Turback

The Timeless Martini
Evolution of the Iconic Cocktail,
with a Century of Recipes and Lore

by Michael Turback

HISTORY
COMPANY
BOOKS

CONTENTS

INTRODUCTION

October, 1906. The Knickerbocker Hotel, a Gilded Age temple built by John Jacob Astor IV, heir to one of America's great fortunes, opened its doors and caused a sensation. Anchored at the southeast corner of Broadway and Forty-Second Street, the Knickerbocker would play host to the world's biggest names in entertainment, politics, culture and high society during the earliest years of the 20th century.

The fourteen-story building in the Beaux-Arts style was faced with red brick and ornamented with terra cotta and Indiana limestone, featuring many exuberant French Renaissance details. The structure was crowned by a three-story, steeply-pitched green copper mansard roof, punctuated with segmental-arched dormer windows and topped with corner urns and cresting. The main dining room, with accommodations for 2,000 patrons, was decorated with tapestries and appointed with electrified fountains, its beamed ceiling modeled after the Chateau de Fontainbleau in Paris. The hotel coddled guests in European-style luxury, including individual "Paris-made" winding clocks in each of its 556 rooms.

"Old King Cole and His Fiddler's Three," a thirty-foot oil painting by painter and illustrator Maxfield Parish, was commissioned by Astor for the Knickerbocker Bar, the grandest watering hole in all New York. Standing at the corner which by then had become the crossroads of the world, the bar established itself as the favorite meeting place of the great and most interesting figures of the city.

According to Knickerbocker chef Louis De Gouy, it was *New York Sun* writer Frank O'Malley who first dubbed the Knickerbocker Bar as the "Forty-Second Street Country Club." One prominent journalist of the era described the "silk-hatted men about town, taking their last before-the-theatre drink while Old King Cole smiled benignly from above."

Amory Blaine, the protagonist in F. Scott Fitzgerald's debut novel, *This Side of Paradise*, famously drank away his sorrows in the Knickerbocker Bar under the watchful eyes of Old King Cole after Amory's girlfriend Rosalind Connage ended their budding relationship. Fitzgerald himself once went on a three-day bender there, "throwing $20 and $50 bills around like so much confetti," according to his biographer Harold Bloom.

In December 1907 the Knickerbocker Bar hosted a wild and memorable party in honor of the hotel's most famous resident, Broadway impresario George M. Cohan. "You couldn't take a look any place without seeing someone," wrote *The New York Sun*. At one table ex-heavyweight champion "Gentleman Jim" Corbett discussed the finer points of writing with novelist and Olympic water polo player Rex Beach. Seated at another table was gunfighter Bat Masterson, the O.K. Corral legend who had become a New York City sportswriter and a man known for his knack at getting questions answered.

One day in 1909, a wild-eyed woman in spectacles and black dress strode into the Knickerbocker Bar and yelled at the top of her lungs, "You are all going to hell!" It was Carrie Nation, the temperance activist famous for smashing up barrooms with an axe.

Today, the Knickerbocker Bar is remembered for its role in the dawn of the modern Martini, mixed behind the grand mahogany counter by Italian immigrant bartender Martini di Arma di Taggia. Mr. Martini played an important role in the evolution of the venerable cocktail when he first married London Dry Gin and Noilly Prat Dry Vermouth, added a dash of orange bitters, then christened the resulting concoction after himself. (It was another Knickerbocker bartender, Robert Agneau, who realized that the one thing the drink most needed to bring the flavors together in transcendent bliss would be, of all things, an olive). This story was reinforced by John Doxat, author of *Drinks and Drinking*, who passed Martini's formula on to another Italian bartender – Luiga of the Savoia Majestic Hotel Bar in Genoa, Italy.

Interestingly, Harry Craddock, who became one of the most influential bartenders of the early-20th century, also plied his trade behind the Knickerbocker Bar, where, it is said, he mixed the last legal drink in America before the country went dry. When Prohibition shuttered the Knick, Craddock set sail for London. During his tour of duty at the Savoy Hotel's American Bar, he helped codify and popularize the Martini that we now know and love. Hat's off to Harry!

By 1934, historian Albert S. Crockett, author of *The Old Waldorf Astoria Bar Book*, reported that "During the first two decades of the century, the commonly accepted American definition of the cocktail was a mixture of gin and vermouth with bitters."

This is not to be taken lightly: The miracle of the Martini, the interplay between gin and vermouth, has become a near religious ritual for some – calibrating ratios, it seems, is more theology than mixology. While some of the earliest attempts were made with equivalent measures of the two ingredients, as the quality of gins improved, the Martini took a journey into dryness, expanding the gin-vermouth ratio from 3-to-1 all the way to 15-to-1 and beyond. Ernest Hemingway called his preferred lubricant the "Montgomery Martini," inspired by British Field Marshal Bernard Montgomery who supposedly refused to go into battle unless his numerical advantage was at least 15-to-1.

Besides Mr. Hemingway, the Martini has had countless devotees, white knights, and evangelists. An American icon, the Martini is an idea, a statement, and, to the faithful, a lifestyle. It is ever-present in literature, film, diplomacy, and pop culture.

E.B. White considered the Martini an "elixir of quietude," and Baltimore satirist H. L. Mencken declared the drink "the only American invention as perfect as the sonnet." Spanish filmmaker Luis Bunuel explained, "To provoke, or sustain, a reverie in a bar, you have to drink English gin, especially in the form of the Dry Martini." Comedian Jackie Gleason, "The Great One," insisted, "A man must defend his home, his wife, his children, and his Martini."

"There is something about a Martini," rhymes Ogden Nash, "Ere the dining and dancing begin; and to tell you the truth, it is not the vermouth – I think that perhaps it's the gin. James Thurber explains, "One Martini is all right. Two are too many, and three are not enough." And on the matter of numbers, Dorothy Parker writes: "I like to have a Martini, two at the very most; after three I'm under the table, after four, I'm under my host."

According to Barnaby Conrad III, "A great Martini should be like skinny-dipping in a Nordic lake with Greta Garbo – teeth chatteringly cold." "This is an excellent Martini," writes Herman Wouk, "sort of tastes like it isn't there at all, just a cold cloud." Somerset Maugham insisted, "Martinis should always be stirred, not shaken, so that the molecules lie sensuously on top of one another." And M.F.K. Fisher, the preeminent food writer, confided that "a well-made Martini or Gibson, correctly chilled and nicely served, has been more often my true friend than any two-legged creature."

After Frederick Henry, Hemingway's alter ego in *A Farewell to Arms*, left the carnage of the First World War, he went to the bar of a grand hotel and ordered a Martini. "The sandwiches came and I ate three and drank a couple more Martinis. I had never tasted anything so cool and clean. They made me feel civilized." A waitress in Kurt Vonnegut Jr.'s novel called a Martini the "breakfast of champions." "I am prepared to believe that a Dry Martini slightly impairs the palate," explained British novelist Alec Waugh, "but think what it does for the soul."

Franklin Roosevelt loved Martinis and is rumored to have carried a "Martini kit" with him wherever he went. FDR plied Stalin with Martinis at the Teheran Conference in 1943, causing Nikita Khrushchev to later declare the Martini "America's lethal weapon."

Lyndon Johnson favored the in-and-out Martini – starting with a glass filled with vermouth, then emptied and filled with gin. Alfred Hitchcock's Martini recipe called for "five parts gin and a quick glance at a bottle of vermouth," while Winston Churchill poured tumblers of freezing gin while bowing in the direction of France. W.C. Fields held a bottle of gin in one hand and a bottle of vermouth in the other, and took alternate pulls, favoring the gin. In the 1958 film *Teacher's Pet*, Clark Gable's character tips a vermouth bottle upside down to wet the cork, then runs the damp cork around the lip of the Martini glass. When told by his doctor to cut back to one Martini a day, legendary saloonkeeper Toots Shor complied by spilling a small amount of gin from a full bottle and topping it off with vermouth.

Drinking companions Charles Butterworth and Nathaniel Benchley invented a game they called "Subway," in which they pushed each other in a wheelbarrow around the swimming pool at the Garden of Allah hotel in West Hollywood. Butterworth delivered his now-famous line after being dumped into the pool during one of their inebriated excursions: "I need to get out of these wet clothes and into a Dry Martini."

In 1972's *The Discreet Charm of the Bourgeoisie*, Luis Bunuel's character advises "a Dry Martini should be sipped like Champagne," and "a classic cone-shaped glass is best." An angular monument to deco design, the characteristic V-shaped bowl and fine stem have represented the Martini since the late 1940s, replacing the coupe of an earlier era. Its widened brim allowing the botanicals of gin to release their complex signature aromatics and graceful, lengthened stem keeping the drinks as cold as possible. Charles Bork of *National Review* writes: "The Martini glass can be seen as an evolutionary (if you believe in that sort of thing) signpost marking the human transition to a higher life form from the lower strata of animal life (and perhaps of vegetable life)." In any case, few symbols are more powerful, more recognizable or more American than the Martini glass.

Dashiell Hammett's Nick Charles insisted on shaking his Martinis "to waltz time." James Bond's drinking habits mirror those of his creator, Ian Fleming, who preferred Martinis shaken, not stirred; Fleming thought that stirring a drink diminished its flavor. Shaking, however, introduces air bubbles into the mix, resulting in a cloudy appearance and a somewhat different texture on the tongue when compared with a stirred drink. Most connoisseurs believe that shaking a Martini is a faux pas, supposedly because the shaking "bruises" the gin (a term referring to a slight bitter taste that can allegedly occur when gin is shaken).

If you serve your Martini with a twist, swipe the inside of each glass with it, to impart some of the lemon's essential oils to the cocktail. Otherwise, just plunk your choice of a stuffed green olive, cocktail onion or a couple drops of bitters into the drink. Sip, but don't nurse. A Martini that has lost its chill has lost much of its appeal.

Novelist, literary critic and spirits connoisseur Kingsley Amis proclaimed, "the Dry Martini is the most famous and the best cocktail in the world." Since its inception at the Knickerbocker Bar, you could say the Martini has become half drink, half art form, combining energy and austerity, power and subtlety, urbanity and sophistication, as bartenders continue to experiment with ways to refine and reinterpret the timeless formula.

The following pages offer an eclectic collection of 88 tried-and-true recipes that explore the evolution of the Martini, from pre- and post-Prohibition classics to inventive contemporary notions developed in progressive cocktail programs.

For you, dear reader, offered is a book's worth of inspiration and guidance. With this volume as trusted accomplice, you're invited to experience and appreciate, in the words of Bernard DeVoto, "the supreme American gift to world culture."

COCKTAILS

MARTINEZ

The past is always the Martini's perfect prologue. This anteced-
ent of the Martini originated with Old Tom Gin, a botanically-
intensive style, rounded by light sweetness. (Its interaction
with sweet vermouth and Maraschino actually suggests a kin-
ship with the Manhattan Cocktail). According to John Walker's
*Bottoms Up: Being a Glossary of Useful Information for the
Thirsty* (5362), George Rector's Hotel Claridge in New York City
was a "turbulent rendezvous for the disciples of the Martinez."

> 1 1/2 ounces Old Tom gin
> 1 1/2 ounces Italian Vermouth
> 1 dash Angostura bitters
> 2 dashes Maraschino liqueur
> lemon peel

Combine liquid ingredients in a mixing glass filled with
cracked ice. Stir briskly and strain into a chilled coupe
glass. Express lemon peel over the glass, rub it around
the rim, and drop it in.

THE PURITAN

By the turn of the last century, European and American palates were becoming accustomed to the refreshing dryness of the new, London-style gins. The Puritan, possibly so named for its austere dryness, appeared in Frederic Lawrence Knowles' 1900 *The Cocktail Book: A Sideboard Manual for Gentlemen,* **among precursors to the Dry Martini.**

        1 1/2 ounces dry gin
        3/4 ounce French vermouth
        1 barspoon Yellow Chartreuse
        3 dashes orange bitters

Combine ingredients in a mixing glass filled with cracked ice. Stir briskly and strain into a chilled coupe glass.

TURF CLUB

A sibling of the Martinez was first concocted at New York's Turf Club, the gentlemen's club on the corner of Madison Avenue and 26th Street, where members gathered to play the horses. Albert Stevens Crockett immortalized this thirst quencher in *The Waldorf-Astoria Bar Book*, writing, "At times a good half – possibly two-thirds – of the crowd in the bar were interested in racing, and would appreciate a cocktail of such a name."

> 2 ounces Holland gin (Genever)
> 1 ounce Italian vermouth
> 1 dash Angostura bitters
> lemon peel

Combine liquid ingredients in a mixing glass filled with cracked ice. Stir briskly and strain into a chilled coupe glass. Express lemon peel over the glass, rub it around the rim, and drop it in.

THE CRISP

John Applegreen, who performed bartending duties at Kinsley's in Chicago and later at the Holland House in New York, advanced the concept of a "Dry Martini," inspired not by ingredient proportions, but with the emergence of the London Dry gin style. The Crisp Cocktail made its first appeared in the 1899 edition of *Applegreen's Bar Book*. He believed the drink should neither taste solely of gin nor vermouth; it ought to be a perfect balance of both.

> 1 3/4 ounces dry gin
> 1 3/4 ounces French vermouth
> 2 dashes of orange bitters
> lemon peel

Combine liquid ingredients in a mixing glass filled with cracked ice. Stir for 10 seconds and strain over new ice in a rocks glass. Express lemon peel over the glass, rub it around the rim, and drop it in.

THE MCCUTCHEON

Among the "invigorators and brain dusters" in *Applegreen's Bar Book*, the McCutcheon cocktail begins where the Crisp Cocktail left off, marrying gin with both sweet and dry vermouths, then christening the drink with the persistent cherry aromatics of Maraschino, one of the oldest European liqueurs.

>1 1/2 ounces dry gin
>3/4 ounce French vermouth
>3/4 ounce Italian vermouth
>1 dash Maraschino liqueur
>1 dash orange bitters

Combine ingredients in a mixing glass filled with cracked ice. Stir briskly and strain into a chilled coupe glass.

HANKY PANKY

In 1903, Ada "Coley" Coleman was promoted to head bartender of the American Bar at the Savoy Hotel in London, one of only two women to have held that position. When actor Charles Hawtrey stopped in for a drink and requested "something with a bit of punch in it," Miss Coleman amplified equal parts gin and sweet vermouth with unapologetic dashes of Fernet-Branca. He took took a sip, then, draining the glass, said, "By Jove! That is the real hanky-panky!" The name stuck.

> 1 1/2 ounces gin
> 1 1/2 ounces Italian vermouth
> 2 dashes Fernet-Branca
> orange peel

Combine liquid ingredients in a mixing glass filled with cracked ice. Stir briskly and strain into a chilled coupe glass. Express orange peel over the glass, rub it around the rim, and drop it in.

ASTORIA

Its name inspired by John Jacob Astor, the era's wealthiest American, the Astoria was conceived by Jacques Straub, manager of the famed Pendennis Club of Louisville, Kentucky, later the wine steward of the Blackstone Hotel in Chicago. In 1914, Straub authored a collection of recipes called *Drinks*, and the Astoria appears among its 700 recipes. His use of Old Tom gin instead of a London dry added sweetness and a softer, mellower quality to the cocktail.

> 1 ounce Old Tom gin
> 2 ounces French vermouth
> 2 dashes orange bitters
> lemon peel

Combine liquid ingredients in a mixing glass filled with cracked ice. Stir briskly and strain into a chilled coupe glass. Express lemon peel over the glass, rub it around the rim, and drop it in.

BLOODHOUND

History holds that it was Thomas Bullock, head bartender at the St. Louis Country Club, who first added fresh fruit to the Martini. Mr. Bullock was the first African-American bartender to publish a cocktail manual, *The Ideal Bartender* in 1917. His recipe was validated in Harry McElhone's *ABC of Cocktails*, then later in *The Savoy Cocktail Book*. Thickness of the muddled strawberries add a syrupy texture to the drink.

> 2 or 3 fresh strawberries
> 1 1/2 ounces dry gin
> 3/4 ounce French Vermouth
> 3/4 ounce Italian Vermouth

Muddle strawberries at the bottom of a mixing glass. Fill with cracked ice and liquid ingredients. Shake vigorously and double strain into a chilled coupe glass.

GIN AND IT

Bon vivant Charles H. Baker, who ate and drank his way around the world during the first quarter of the 20th century, chronicled his adventure in the two-volume *Gentleman's Companion*. In it, he affirmed the importance of gin: "No bar can be without dry gin and be called a bar." The "It" in this minimalist recipe is sweet (Italian) Vermouth, and in Baker's words, "the wetter the better." The libation is sometimes called Gin and Cin after Cinzano, a popular brand of Italian Sweet Vermouth.

    1 1/2 ounces dry gin
    1 1/2 ounces Italian vermouth

Combine ingredients in a mixing glass filled with cracked ice. Stir briskly and strain into a chilled coupe glass.

CORNELL
COCKTAIL

In *The Old Waldorf-Astoria Bar Book*, Albert Crockett calls this drink "a compliment to an institution at Ithaca, many of whose alumni – mining engineers and others – used it to toast Alma Mater." If you splash in some orange bitters, the Cornell becomes a Dewey; if you add a squeeze of orange peel to a Dewey, you've got a Racquet Club, which, with Italian vermouth and a dash of Angostura, answers to the name of Hearst.

> 1 1/2 ounces dry gin
> 1 1/2 ounces French vermouth

Combine ingredients in a mixing glass filled with cracked ice. Stir briskly and strain into a chilled coupe glass.

PRINCETON COCKTAIL

It was George Kappeler, head bartender at New York's Holland House Hotel, who attached the names of Ivy League institutions to a few of his original cocktails. Heavy and rich, port lends not only flavor to this drink, but when poured into the coupe glass with a steady hand, the wine settles on the bottom, creating a two-tone visual effect.

> 2 ounces Old Tom gin
> 2 dashes orange bitters
> 3/4 ounce ruby port, chilled
> lemon peel

Combine gin and bitters in a mixing glass filled with cracked ice. Stir briskly and strain into a chilled coupe glass. Gently pour the port into the glass, allowing it to slide down the side and settle on the bottom of the drink. Express lemon peel over the glass, rub it around the rim, and discard.

YALE COCKTAIL

The 1906 Yale Bulldogs football team finished with a 9-0-1 record and was named national champion. That same year, students devised a cocktail using Blue Curacao to mimic the school color. Alumni embraced the drink which has endured many variations of the standard formula. This recipe is accepted as the standard.

> 1 1/2 ounces dry gin
> 1/2 ounce French vermouth
> 1 teaspoon Blue Curacao
> 1 dash orange bitters
> lemon peel

Combine liquid ingredients in a mixing glass filled with cracked ice. Stir briskly and strain into a chilled coupe glass. Express lemon peel over the glass, rub it around the rim, and drop it in.

BRONX

A drink that has fallen out of favor since its heyday, the Bronx is essentially a "Perfect" Martini with a complement of orange juice. (Historian Bernard DeVoto claimed that fruit juice in a Martini is "pure poison"). The citrusy cocktail was created by Johnnie Solan, legendary pre-Prohibition bartender at New York City's Waldorf-Astoria.

> 1 1/2 ounces dry gin
> 1/2 ounce Italian vermouth
> 1/2 ounce French vermouth
> 3/4 ounce orange juice, fresh
> orange peel

Combine liquid ingredients in a mixing glass filled with cracked ice. Stir briskly and strain into a chilled coupe glass. Express orange peel over the glass, rub it around the rim, and drop it in.

ABBEY MARTINI

President of the United Kingdom Bartender's Guild, William J. Tarling compiled *The Cafe Royal Cocktail Book*, one of the literary gems of the gilded age of cocktails. Cafe Royal was a place where American spirits mixed with European liqueurs and aperitifs in astounding ways, reflecting the glamor and decadence of pre-war England. Tarling's Abbey Martini is closely related to the better-known Bronx.

> 2 ounces dry gin
> 1 ounce Lillet
> 1 ounce orange juice, fresh
> 3 dashes Angostura bitters
> orange peel

Combine liquid ingredients in a mixing glass filled with cracked ice. Stir briskly and strain into a chilled coupe glass. Express orange peel over the glass, rub it around the rim, and drop it in.

ZAZA

A play by French authors Pierre Berton and Charles Simon, *Zaza* was adapted by David Belasco and produced in America in 1898. The title character (played by Leslie Carter, "The American Sarah Bernhardt") is a prostitute who becomes a music hall entertainer and the mistress of a married man. Zaza captured the imagination of New York bartender Hugo Ensslin who included this appreciation in 1916's Recipes for Mixed Drinks.

> 1 1/2 ounces dry gin
> 1 1/2 ounces Dubonnet Rouge
> 1 dash Angostura bitters
> lemon peel

Combine liquid ingredients in a mixing glass filled with cracked ice. Stir briskly and strain into a chilled coupe glass. Express lemon peel over the glass, rub it around the rim, and drop it in.

SKINNER & EDDY

The road to the Dry Martini is paved with the odd and the eccentric. According to "Luscious" Lucius Beebe (moniker bestowed by Walter Winchell), Crosby Gaige was never known to shy away "when the ice in the shaker called stirringly to duty." His eccentric gin-based cocktail is named in honor of Ned Skinner and John Eddy, World War I shipbuilders, notable for breaking world production speed records for ship construction.

> 1 ounce dry gin
> 3/4 ounce Yellow Chartreuse
> 2 dashes orange bitters

Combine ingredients in a mixing glass filled with cracked ice. Stir briskly and strain into a coupe glass.

JUPITER MARTINI

Parfait Amour is a mixological curiosity, a centuries-old French liqueur that made its way into speakeasy Martinis during Prohibition. Since the quality of gin in dry America was often questionable, bartenders added all manner of sweet ingredients to mask the flavor. Parfait Amour imparted fruity and spicy notes of orange and vanilla to the Jupiter.

> 1 1/2 ounces dry gin
> 3/4 ounce French vermouth
> 1 barspoon Parfait Amour
> 1 barspoon orange juice
> orange peel

Combine liquid ingredients in a mixing glass filled with cracked ice. Shake vigorously and strain into a chilled coupe glass. Express orange peel over the glass, rub it around the rim, and drop it in.

HARRY'S COCKTAIL

Bartender Harry MacElhone acquired Harry's New York Bar in Paris in 1923. A year later, together with the journalist O.O. McEntyre, he organized a group called the International Bar Flies, an organization for serious drinkers with its own secret handshake and a necktie featuring a fly on a lump of sugar. Harry's became a magnet for Americans who traveled to Paris for drinks including a drink Harry named after himself.

> 2 ounces dry gin
> 1 ounce Italian vermouth
> 1 dash absinthe
> fresh mint sprig

Combine liquid ingredients in a mixing glass filled with cracked ice. Shake vigorously and strain into a chilled coupe glass. Garnish with mint sprig.

ALASKA
COCKTAIL

"So far as can be ascertained," explains Harry Craddock in *The Savoy Cocktail Book* (1930), "this delectable potion is NOT the staple diet of the Esquimaux. It was probably first thought of in South Carolina – hence its name." In 1948's *The Fine Art of Mixing Drinks*, David Embury adds a measure of dry sherry to create an Alaska spinoff called the "Nome." Brrr!

> 1 1/2 ounces dry gin
> 1/2 ounce Yellow Chartreuse
> 1 dash orange bitters
> lemon peel

Combine liquid ingredients in a mixing glass filled with cracked ice. Stir briskly and strain into a chilled coupe glass. Express lemon peel over the glass, rub it around the rim, and drop it in.

BIJOU

Legendary barman Harry Johnson likely named this drink for colors of three jewels (*bijous* in French): gin for the diamond, vermouth the ruby, and Chartreuse the emerald – three components that come together agreeably for a refreshing and balanced cocktail. The original recipe called for equal parts gin, vermouth, and Chartreuse, but contemporary adaptations tame both vermouth and Chartreuse. (In Paris, the Ritz Bar version bid *au revoir* to Chartruese, partnering gin with orange curacao and dry vermouth). Its combination of gin, sweet vermouth, and Chartreuse is a classic mini-lesson in late nineteenth-century cocktailing.

> 2 ounces dry gin
> 1 ounce Green Chartreuse
> 1 ounce Italian vermouth
> 1 dash orange bitters
> lemon peel

Combine liquid ingredients in a mixing glass filled with cracked ice. Shake vigorously and strain into a chilled coupe glass. Express lemon peel over the glass, rub it around the rim, and drop it in.

THE ALBERTO

Dry, complex and aromatic, this drink appeared in W. J. Tarling's 1937 *Café Royal Cocktail Book*, its invention credited to A. J. Smith, a member in good standing of the United Kingdom Bartender's Guild. On the importance of mixology, Mr. Tarling writes, "In the morning the merchant, the lawyer, or the Methodist deacon takes his cocktail. Suppose it is not properly compounded? The whole day's proceedings go crooked because the man himself feels wrong from the effects of an unskillfully mixed drink."

    1 1/4 ounces dry gin
    1 1/4 ounces Lillet
    1 ounce dry sherry
    1 dash of Cointreau
    orange peel

Combine liquid ingredients in a mixing glass filled with cracked ice. Stir briskly and strain into a chilled coupe glass. Express orange peel over the glass, rub it around the rim, and drop it in.

GIBSON

Improvised by bartender Charley Connolly of the Players Club for "Gibson Girl" illustrator Charles Dana Gibson, the Gibson Cocktail lends a whisper of savory and umami undertone to the Martini with a pickled cocktail onion in place of the typical briny olive. In 1957, *Esquire Magazine* compiled a list of celebrity thirst quenchers in Drink Book, including this onion-laden Gibson courtesy of Guy Lombardo, whose orchestra played at the Roosevelt Hotel in New York City.

> 2 ounces dry gin
> 1/2 ounce French vermouth
> 6 pearl onions

Combine liquid ingredients in a mixing glass filled with cracked ice. Stir briskly and strain into a chilled Martini glass. Drop onions into the glass.

FIFTH AVENUE

Before the onset of Prohibition, the last legal cocktail in America is said to have been mixed at the old Holland House on New York's Fifth Avenue by Harry Craddock, one of the most influential mixologists of the early-20th century. Before he set off for London to resume tending bar at the Savoy Hotel, Mr. Craddock created a bracing libation, immortalized in the *Esquire Drink Book*, and named for its birthplace.

> 1 1/2 ounces dry gin
> 3/4 ounce Italian vermouth
> 3/4 ounce Fernet-Branca

Combine ingredients in a mixing glass filled with cracked ice. Shake vigorously and strain into a chilled coupe glass.

ATTENTION

The Attention made its first appearance in Hugo Ensslin's *Recipes for Mixed Drinks* in 5351. It then reappeared under an abridged moniker, the Atty, in the 1930 *Savoy Cocktail Book*. In the latter rendition, author and bartender Harry Craddock edited the drink to proportions more accessible for a modern palate, essentially creating a fancier Martini.

> 1/4 ounce absinthe
> 2 ounces dry gin
> 1 ounce French vermouth
> 1 barspoon crème de violette
> 2 dashes orange bitters
> lemon peel

Combine liquid ingredients in a mixing glass filled with cracked ice. Stir for 10 seconds and strain into a coupe glass. Express lemon peel over the glass, rub it around the rim, and drop it in.

SO-SO MARTINI

This well intentioned re-working of the Martini, invented by Mr. P. Soso, manager of the Kit Kat Club in London, was an opportunity to introduce a layer of apple from the Calvados, yet the doubling-up of vermouth and grenadine results in an overly sweet wallop. Unfortunately, the drink lives up to its name.

> 1 ounce dry gin
> 1 ounce Italian vermouth
> 1/2 ounce calvados
> 4 dashes grenadine syrup
> apple slice

Combine liquid ingredients in a mixing glass filled with cracked ice. Stir briskly and strain into a chilled coupe glass. Garnish with apple slice.

ATTA BOY COCKTAIL

Almost every craft cocktail bar in London – and probably the world – has a well-thumbed copy of Harry Craddock's *The Savoy Cocktail Book* on the back bar, as this collection of more than 144 recipes remains, 83 years after its publication, an incredible influence on London's bartenders. Craddock employs notes of pomegranate from the grenadine, adding complexity to the Martini archetype. Atta boy!

> 2 ounces dry gin
> 1 ounce French vermouth
> 1/3 ounce grenadine syrup
> orange peel

Combine ingredients in a mixing glass filled with cracked ice. Shake vigorously and strain into a chilled coupe glass. Express orange peel over the glass, rub it around the rim, and drop it in.

BARRY COCKTAIL

There's a strong tie between the Barry and other flirtations with the Martini formula during Prohibition, this version distinguished by a hint of mint. In 1929, Charles H. Baker Jr. first met "Barry" at the Army & Navy Club in Manila, Philippines. Like all proper Martinis, according to Mr. Baker, the drink "must be cold indeed."

2 ounces dry gin
1 ounce Italian vermouth
1 dash Angostura bitters
1/2 teaspoon white crème de menthe

Add gin, vermouth, and bitters to a mixing glass filled with cracked ice. Stir briskly and strain into a chilled coupe glass. Float crème de menthe by holding a teaspoon bottom-side up over the glass and pouring the liqueur slowly over it.

ROLLS-ROYCE

The drink first shows up in *The Savoy Cocktail Book*, the brain-child of Harry Craddock. Born in the UK, Craddock came of age behind the bar at New York's famed Knickerbocker and Hoffman House hotels, before becoming the best-known bartender at London's American Bar in the Savoy Hotel. Craddock likely created the Rolls-Royce cocktail, catering to the Bright Young Things of London society who congregated at the American Bar.

> 1/4 ounce Benedictine
> 1 1/2 ounces dry gin
> 3/4 ounce French vermouth
> 3/4 ounce Italian vermouth
> lemon peel

Fill a Martini glass with ice and let it sit until the glass is chilled. Once the glass is chilled, toss the ice, pour in Benedictine, swirl it around to fully coat the interior walls of the glass, then discard. Combine gin, and vermouths in a mixing glass filled with cracked ice. Stir briskly and strain into the prepared glass. Express lemon peel over the glass, rub it around the rim, and drop it in.

COLONY COCKTAIL

The Colony, rendezvous of New York high society, remained open through the "dry" years of Prohibition, hiding the liquor stash in an elevator as a precaution against raids by enforcement agents. Marco Hattem, the Colony's head bartender, is credited with not only devising the house cocktail, but, while stirring Martinis was the nearly universal custom, he insisted on a vigorous shake.

> 1 1/2 ouncesdry gin
> 3/4 ounce grapefruit juice, fresh
> 2 teaspoon Maraschino liqueur

Combine ingredients in a mixing glass filled with cracked ice. Shake vigorously and strain into a chilled coupe glass.

NAPOLÉON

"Glory is fleeting," said Napoléon Bonaparte, "but obscurity is forever." Italian barmen have revived this forgotten relic from Harry Craddock's 1930 *Savoy Cocktail Book*, enhancing the pleasant bitterness of wine-based Dubonnet with an adventurous dash of Fernet-Branca. Dubonnet was popularized during World War I by the British Queen Mother who sipped Craddock's Zaza Cocktail (Dubonnet and gin) every day at lunch.

> 2 ounces dry gin
> 1/4 ounce Dubonnet Rouge
> 1 ounce orange curacao
> 1 dash Fernet-Branca
> lemon peel

Combine liquid ingredients in a mixing glass filled with cracked ice. Stir briskly and strain into a chilled coupe glass. Express lemon peel over the glass, rub it around the rim, and drop it in.

SATAN'S
WHISKERS

This cocktail emerged from the Embassy Club, a Hollywood speakeasy run by impresario Adolph "Eddie" Brandstatter. It is said that wherever Eddie was, that was the party. Satan's Whiskers is a variation on the Bronx, first appearing in print in Harry Craddock's *Savoy Cocktail Book* from 1930. (The drink can be made in two ways – either "straight" with Grand Marnier, or "curled" with Orange Curaçao).

> 1/2 ounce dry gin
> 1/2 ounce Grand Marnier
> 1/2 ounce Italian vermouth
> 1/2 ounce French vermouth
> 1/2 ounce orange juice, fresh
> 1 dash orange bitters
> orange peel

Combine liquid ingredients in a mixing glass filled with cracked ice. Shake vigorously and strain into a chilled Martini glass. Express orange peel over the glass, rub it around the rim, and drop it in.

TUXEDO

Its name refers to Tuxedo Park, at one time a refuge for Gilded Age high society and birthplace of the tail-less suit, called, yes, the tuxedo. Before shuffling out of the city after work, Tuxedoites regularly stopped off at the city's top bars, most notable among them the Waldorf-Astoria bar, where this relative of the Martini was born. The drink was immortalized by Albert Stevens Crockett in 1931's *Old Waldorf Bar Days*.

> 2 ounces dry gin
> 1 ounce fino sherry
> 2 dashes orange bitters
> orange peel

Combine liquid ingredients in a mixing glass filled with cracked ice. Stir briskly and strain into a chilled coupe glass. Express orange peel over the glass, rub it around the rim, and drop it in.

COOPERSTOWN

In *The Stork Club Bar Book*, Lucius Beebe imbeds this drink among the "less exotic but nonetheless popular noontime cocktails" served at the bar, a "perfect" version of the Martini, using equal parts of both sweet and dry vermouth. Skip the mint and add a shot of Cognac for an Astor Painless Anesthetic, the Stork's hangover cure, devised by actress Mary Astor (Brigid O'Shaughnessy in *The Maltese Falcon*).

> 1 1/2 ounces dry gin
> 1/2 ounce French vermouth
> 1/2 ounce Italian vermouth
> 2 sprigs fresh mint

Combine liquid ingredients in a mixing glass filled with cracked ice. Shake and strain into a chilled Martini glass. Garnish with mint sprigs.

THE HANNIGAN

He was the twinkle-eyed, ebony-haired confidant of Sherman Billingsley and the mastermind of the Stork Club's in-house publicity team. Steve Hannagan put his shrewd marketing sense at Billingsley's disposal, hiring a regular club photographer to immortalize guests and luring pretty girls to the club with free Champagne, pins, cosmetics, lucky pennies, and souvenir storks. His signature drink was described by Lucius Beebe as a "particularly lethal Martini.

> 1 1/2 ounces dry gin
> 1/2 ounce dry sherry
> lemon peel

Combine liquid ingredients in a mixing glass filled with cracked ice. Stir briskly and strain into a chilled coupe glass. Express lemon peel over the glass, rub it around the rim, and drop it in.

DON'T GIVE UP
THE SHIP

According to "Luscious" Lucius Beebe (moniker bestowed by Walter Winchell), Crosby Gaige was never known to shy away "when the ice in the shaker called stirringly to duty." His eccentric gin-based cocktail, invigorated with whispers of flavors and aromatics, is offered in Mr. Gaige's 1941 *Cocktail Guide and Ladies Companion*, described as a serious study of the thoughts of the leading bartenders of his era.

1 1/2 ounces dry gin
1 dash Fernet-Branca
1 dash orange curacao
1 dash Dubonnet Rouge
lemon peel

Combine liquid ingredients in a mixing glass filled with cracked ice. Shake vigorously and strain into a chilled coupe glass. Express lemon peel over the glass, rub it around the rim, and drop it in.

CLUB COCKTAIL

The Gin and It cocktail is short for Gin and Italian, a reference to the Italian sweet vermouth. It's one of the oldest Martini drinks, dating back to the 19th century with many variations, none quite as successful as the simple equation put forward by Bill Kelly in his 1945 book *The Roving Bartender*. Kelly calls for the addition of Yellow Chartreuse, and perhaps just as important is how Kelly serves the drink – as a cocktail to be poured straight up.

> 1 ounce dry gin
> 1/2 ounce Italian vermouth
> 1/4 ounce Yellow Chartreuse
> 1 dash orange bitters
> lemon peel

Combine liquid ingredients in a mixing glass filled with cracked ice. Stir briskly and strain into a chilled coupe glass. Express lemon peel over the glass, rub it around the rim, and drop it in.

DIRTY MARTINI

In February 1945, when Franklin Roosevelt met with Joseph Stalin and Winston Churchill in Tehran, Iran to plan a second front against Nazi Germany, he served his favorite drink, a salty invention that adds olive brine to an otherwise standard Martini. (The brine should be added before the cocktail is shaken or stirred, not after it's poured into the glass). Extra olives may be added to amplify the flavor.

> 2 1/2 ounces dry gin
> 1/2 ounce olive brine
> 1/4 ounce French vermouth
> 3 green olives

Combine liquid ingredients in a mixing glass filled with cracked ice. Stir briskly and strain into a chilled Martini glass. Drop olives into the glass.

VODKATINI

During the 1940s, El Morocco's photographer, Jerome Zerbe, spent most nights from 9 PM to 4 AM at the club, where, in his words, "I invented a thing which has become a pain in the neck for most people. I took photographs of the fashionable people and sent them to the papers." Besides pioneering celebrity photography, he was the first to suggest the Martini-inspired mix of vodka and dry vermouth, a drink that began as a society tipple and primed American palates for vodka during World War II.

> 2 ounces vodka
> 1/2 ounce French vermouth
> green olive

Combine liquid ingredients in a mixing glass filled with cracked ice. Shake vigorously and strain into a chilled coupe glass. Drop olive into the glass.

KANGAROO

The faithful would never consider a Martini made with Vodka to be a Martini, hence the Kangaroo, the name David Embry gave to a Martini with vodka in 1948's *The Fine Art of Mixing Drinks*. While the drink was a favorite of Dashiell Hammett, it was Ian Fleming's James Bond who did the most to popularize the drink when he uttered the famous line, "Vodka Martini, shaken, not stirred" in *Goldfinger* in 1959.

> 3 ounces vodka
> 1/2 ounce French vermouth
> lemon peel

Combine liquid ingredients in a mixing glass filled with cracked ice. Shake and strain into a chilled Martini glass. Express lemon peel over the glass, rub it around the rim, and drop it in.

THE OPPENHEIMER

J. Robert Oppenheimer is credited with being the "father of the atomic bomb" for his role in the Manhattan Project, the World War II undertaking that developed the first nuclear weapons used in the atomic bombings of Hiroshima and Nagasaki. Due to the difficulty of getting supplies to his remote Los Alamos lab, Oppenheimer crafted his own Martini recipe that used only a dash of vermouth, as well as lime and honey.

> 4 ounces dry gin
> 1 dash French vermouth
> lime juice, fresh
> honey

Combine gin and vermouth in a mixing glass filled with cracked ice. Stir briskly and strain into a chilled Martini glass whose rim has been dipped in equal parts lime and honey.

TRADER VIC'S
RUM MARTINI

Tiki cocktails have, traditionally, always used rum in some form or another. It was Victor Jules Bergeron, creator of Trader Vic's restaurants, who popularized an astonishing number of exotic, rum-based drinks, including the Mai Tai, Scorpion, and Zombie. In his 1946 *Book of Food and Drink*, Bergeron used the versatile template of the classic Martini, replacing gin with – you guessed it.

> 1 1/2 ounces rum
> 1 ounce French vermouth
> 1 dash orange bitters
> lemon peel

Combine liquid ingredients in a mixing glass filled with cracked ice. Shake and strain into a chilled Martini glass. Express lemon peel over the glass, rub it around the rim, but do not drop.

GUNGA GIN

Ted Shane's "Authentic and Hilarious" *Bar Guide* was published by *True Magazine* in 1950, "dedicated to folks who value their lives, friends, futures, homes, and taste buds, and like to shake up a few for conviviality's sake." Introducing this entry, Mr. Shane explains, "How the chapter got its title and Kipling learned to kipple."

> 1 1/3 ounces dry gin
> 1 1/3 ounces Italian vermouth
> sprig of mint

Combine liquid ingredients in a mixing glass filled with cracked ice. Shake vigorously and strain into a chilled Martini glass. Garnish with mint sprig.

BANANAS FOSTER MARTINI

It's part of the culinary culture of New Orleans. As a dessert, the luscious dish was hatched in 1951 at legendary Brennan's Restaurant. The creamy combination of bananas and Rum is transformed into a cocktail at another Brennan family restaurant, Ralph's on the Park, where it's called a "Martini" and is strained into a Martini glass – but it's still decadent enough to serve as dessert.

1 1/2 ounces Absolut Vanilla Vodka
1 dash spiced rum
1 ounce créme de banana
1/2 ounce butterscotch schnapps
1 splash fresh cream
ground nutmeg

Combine liquid ingredients in a mixing glass filled with cracked ice. Shake and strain into a chilled Martini glass. Dust with nutmeg.

VESPER

The spiritous wallop of vodka and gin first appeared in Ian Fleming's 1953 novel *Casino Royale* when James Bond asked for "Three measures of Gordon's, one of vodka, half a measure of Kina Lillet. Mr. Bond may have recommended shaking it, but please, do stir. It will maintain the silky texture of an all-spirits drink.

>   3 ounces vodka
>   1 ounce dry gin
>   1/2 ounce Lillet Blanc
>   lemon peel

Combine liquid ingredients in a mixing glass filled with cracked ice. Stir briskly and strain into a chilled Martini glass. Express lemon peel over the glass, rub it around the rim, and drop it in.

ARNAUD MARTINI

The recipe, included in the 1955 *Anthology of Cocktails*, was developed by Booth's Gin, in honor of French-born pianist, singer and actress Yvonne Arnaud. The cocktail was first called a "Parisian," yet became more commonly accepted as the Arnaud. The drink is the offspring of mating a Dry Martini with flavors of blackcurrant, falling on the sweet end of the Martini spectrum.

1 ounce dry gin
1 ounce French vermouth
1 ounce crème de cassis
3 fresh blackberries

Combine liquid ingredients in a mixing glass filled with cracked ice. Stir briskly and strain into a chilled Martini glass. Drop blackberries into the glass.

FLYING
DUTCHMAN

It's worth remembering a legend. This drink is named for the ghost ship that can never make port and is doomed to sail the oceans forever. The myth originated from 17th century nautical folklore, and the orange-forward Martini was derived from an obscure 1950s Dutch cocktail book.

>   2 ounces dry gin
>   1 barspoon Triple Sec
>   orange peel

Combine liquid ingredients in a mixing glass filled with cracked ice. Stir briskly and strain into a chilled Martini glass. Express orange peel over the glass, rub it around the rim, and drop it in.

WOLFGANG MARTINI

Named for the German Colonel who organized the *Luft-nachrichtentruppe* (Air Signal Corps) and was largely responsible for promoting early radar development during World War II. Beginning with the formation of the West German armed forces, Martini served as a civilian advisor with the new Air Force in 1956, and later with NATO. Notes of caraway distinguish the German-influenced Martini.

> 1 1/2 ounces dry gin
> 3/4 ounce Kümmel
> 2 dashes French vermouth
> lemon peel

Combine liquid ingredients in a mixing glass filled with cracked ice. Stir briskly and strain into a chilled coupe glass. Express lemon peel over the glass, rub it around the rim, and drop it in.

KNOCKOUT

Cozier bedfellows than gin and vermouth are hard to find. In 1957's *Esquire Drink Book*, equal measures of the two chummy ingredients are joined by Pernod, whose flavor is derived from a distillation of star anise and aromatic plants and herbs. In boxing, the knockout punch requires three elements – power, accuracy, and surprise.

> 1 ounce dry gin
> 1 ounce French vermouth
> 1 ounce Pernod
> 1 fresh mint sprig

Combine liquid ingredients in a mixing glass filled with cracked ice. Stir briskly and strain into a chilled Martini glass. Garnish with mint sprig.

SPACEMAN

British bartender Eddie Clark, who served posts at the Berkeley Hotel, the Savoy Hotel, and the Albany Club, authored _Shaking in the 60s_, a guide to entertaining in "Swinging London," referring to the cultural and social changes that took place in the city during that decade. The emerging Space Age inspired the name of his Vodka Martini.

> 1 1/2 ounces vodka
> 1/2 ounce French vermouth
> 1 dash grenadine syrup
> 1 dash Pernod

Combine ingredients in a mixing glass filled with cracked ice. Stir briskly and strain into a chilled Martini glass.

THE LUCKY JIM

In *Kingsley Amis On Drink* (1970), the grand old man of English letters devised this derivative of the Vodka Martini. "What you serve should be treated with respect," he writes, "not because it is specially strong but because it tastes specially mild and bland." For visual reasons, he suggests leaving the peel on the cucumber slice you float on top.

> 2 1/2 ounces vodka
> 1/4 ounce French vermouth
> 1/4 ounce cucumber juice, fresh
> cucumber slice

Combine liquid ingredients in a mixing glass filled with cracked ice. Shake vigorously and strain into a chilled Martini glass. Garnish with cucumber slice.

BLUE MARTINI

The Blue Bar (named for the blues music playing overhead) is one of the more historically significant bars in New York. Opened in 1933 following the demise of Prohibition, Blue Bar regulars included writers Sinclair Lewis, Dorothy Parker, and actor John Barrymore. The bar was featured in *Mad Men* as one of protagonist Don Draper's favorite spots, where he may have sipped this 1960s-era Blue Martini.

> 2 ounces vodka
> 1/2 ounce blue curacao
> 1/2 ounce lime juice
> lime peel

Combine liquid ingredients in a mixing glass filled with cracked ice. Shake vigorously and strain into a chilled Martini glass. Express lime peel over the glass, rub it around the rim, and drop it in.

NEWPORT

At times during the centuries-long onward march, bartenders have tinkered endlessly with basic Martini components, most notably rearranging ratios of gin to vermouth and dry vermouth to sweet vermouth in an effort to elevate the drink to crowd-pleasing heights. The Newport goes boldly where no Martini has gone before.

> 1 1/4 ounces dry gin
> 1 1/4 ounces French vermouth
> 3/4 ounce Italian vermouth
> orange peel

Combine liquid ingredients in a mixing glass filled with cracked ice. Stir briskly and strain into a chilled Martini glass. Express orange peel over the glass, rub it around the rim, and drop it in.

FLAME OF LOVE

Chasen's was a West Hollywood watering hole, long cherished as a celebrity hangout. The Flame of Love was first crafted behind the horseshoe-shaped bar by bartender Pepe Ruiz in 1970 for one of the bar's famous regulars, Dean Martin, and was purportedly such a hit that Frank Sinatra once celebrated his birthday by ordering a round for everyone in the restaurant.

> 1/4 ounce fino sherry
> 2 ounces vodka
> 2 dashes orange bitters
> several large strips of orange peel

Rinse a chilled Martini glass with sherry and discard excess. While squeezing a large strip of orange peel over the sherry-rinsed glass, use a match to carefully flame the oils spraying into the glass; repeat several times with additional peels. Add vodka and orange bitters to a mixing glass filled with cracked ice and stir briskly, then strain into the prepared glass. Flame a final orange peel over the finished drink.

BIKINI MARTINI

At one time, British drinking habits did not extend far beyond a pint at the pub and an occasional gin and tonic. Then along came Dick Bradsell, considered the father of the cocktail revival that took root in London in the 1990s. Mr. Bradsell plied his trade at Zanzibar, Soho Brasserie, Fred's Club, and most notably at Pink Chihuahua where he created this cocktail for an Agent Provocateur swimwear launch.

> 2 ounces dry gin
> 1/4 ounce Peachtree Liqueur
> 3/4 ounce blue curacao
> 1/4 ounce lemon juice, fresh
> orange peel

Combine liquid ingredients in a mixing glass filled with cracked ice. Shake vigorously and strain into a chilled Martini glass. Express orange peel over the glass, rub it around the rim, and drop it in.

CAJUN MARTINI

Louisiana chef Paul Prudhomme profoundly influenced American cuisine, creating an appetite for Creole and Cajun cooking. Along with andouille gumbos and hotly seasoned finfish, K-Paul's Louisiana Kitchen, his restaurant in the French Quarter of New Orleans, served the chef's exuberant version of the Martini, infusing gin with the heat of jalapeño peppers.

> 2 1/2 ounces jalapeño pepper-infused dry gin*
> 1/4 ounce French vermouth
> red jalapeno pepper

Combine liquid ingredients in a mixing glass filled with cracked ice. Stir briskly and strain into a chilled Martini glass. Drop pepper into the glass.

*Placed a chopped jalapeño pepper into a 750-ml bottle of gin for 12 hours to infuse.

FLIRTINI

A Martini only by a long stretch of the imagination, this iconic drink was developed for *Sex and the City* actress Sarah Jessica Parker by a bartender at Guastavino's in New York City. This pink, fruity, feminine drink is most often mixed for a girls-night-in or bachelorette party.

> 1 ounce vodka
> 2 ounces pineapple juice
> Champagne, chilled

Combine vodka and pineapple juice in a mixing glass filled with cracked ice. Shake vigorously and strain into a chilled Martini glass. Top up with Champagne.

CHOCOLATE MARTINI

In the spirit of experimentation, bartender Eamon Rockey of New York's Betony combines crème de cacao with vodka and nutty amontillado sherry. The unorthodox addition of the dry Spanish wine to a base of vodka balances his crème de cacao's chocolatey flavor profile and velvety texture.

> 1 1/2 ounces vodka
> 1 ounce crème de cacao
> 1 ounce amontillado sherry
> cocoa powder

Combine liquid ingredients in a mixing glass with cracked ice. Shake vigorously and strain into a chilled Martini glass. Dust with cocoa.

FRENCH MARTINI

Modeled after a quintessential Parisian brasserie, New York's Balthazar has high-backed red leather banquettes, scarred and peeling brass oversize mirrors, high tin ceiling, scuffed tiled floor, faded saffron yellow walls, large windows, and antique lighting. It has become an institution in the city that surrounds it. The French Martini was invented for the restaurant's opening in 1997.

> 2 ounces vodka
> 1/2 ounce Chambord
> 2 1/2 ounces pineapple juice

Combine ingredients in a mixing glass filled with cracked ice. Shake vigorously and strain into a chilled Martini glass.

ESPRESSO MARTINI

Richard Arthur "Dick" Bradsell has been described as one part Jeeves, one part Lloyd from *The Shining*, and one part eccentric schoolmaster – with a dash of surrealist poet. He turned cocktail-making into an art, instinctively knowing how to blend, balance and pair tastes to make a perfect drink, the way a master parfumier knows how to make a scent. He famously created this drink at the request of a supermodel who asked for something that would, "Wake her up, then fuck her up."

> 3/4 ounce coffee liqueur
> 1 1/2 ounces vodka
> 1 ounce fresh espresso
> 3 whole coffee beans

Combine liquid ingredients in a mixing glass with cracked ice. Shake vigorously and strain into a chilled Martini glass. Drop coffee beans into the glass.

JULIA CHILD UPSIDE-DOWN MARTINI

Famous for popularizing French cuisine in the American kitchen, Julia Child improvised her own aperitif, essentially a Martini that's heavier on the vermouth than gin, closer in spirit to the way dry vermouth is consumed in Europe. Her recipe calls for a 5 to 1 ratio of Noilly Prat vermouth (her favorite) to gin, stirred with ice. As she said of her creation, "It's a nice refreshing drink. I usually have two."

> 2 1/2 ounces French vermouth
> 1/2 ounce dry gin
> lemon peel

In a white wine glass filled with ice, stir together gin and vermouth. Express lemon peel over the glass, rub it around the rim, and drop it in.

HARRY DENTON MARTINI

In San Francisco, they say it's not a party unless Harry Denton is there. A man *The San Francisco Chronicle* calls one of the city's most visible bon vivants, and promoter and owner of several successful establishments, including The Starlight Club atop the St. Francis Hotel, Denton once explained, "The bar is the grandest stage in the world and the bartender brings it to life every night." His Martini has become a San Francisco classic.

> 1 1/4 ounces dry gin
> 1/2 ounce Green Chartreuse

Combine ingredients in a mixing glass filled with cracked ice. Shake vigorously and strain into a chilled Martini glass.

MARGATINI

It's a cross between a Martini and a Margarita, invented during the early 1990s at Handsome Harry's in Naples, Florida. Tequila adds depth and spark, while savory flavors of pineapple and pomegranate counteract tart, slightly bitter notes of the native, thin-skinned limes. Somerset Maugham declared that "Martinis should always be stirred, not shaken, so that the molecules lie sensuously one on top of the other." Harry doesn't agree.

2 ounces tequila
1 ounce pineapple juice
1 ounce pomegranate juice
1/2 ounce key lime juice
key lime slice

Combine liquid ingredients in a a mixing glass filled with cracked ice. Shake vigorously and strain into a sugar-rimmed coupe. Garnish with key lime.

ENGLISH MARTINI

Elder is one of those plants surrounded by mystery, magic, and superstition. In old England, it was believed that one could see witches if elder juice was smeared around their eyes. Pregnant Celtic women would kiss the elder to ensure their babies would have good fortune. Nothing screams English more than gin and elderflower, and in 2003, mixologists of the Millennium Hotel combined good old English gin with elderflower liqueur for a Martini reminiscent of tea parties and village fetes.

> 2 1/2 ounces dry gin
> 1 ounce St. Germain Elderflower Liqueur
> 2 rosemary sprigs

Combine the gin and 1 rosemary sprig into a mixing glass and muddle to release the rosemary flavors. Add ice cube and the elderflower liqueur and stir gently. Double-strain into a chilled Martini glass and garnish with the remaining rosemary sprig.

EARL GREY "MARTEANI"

Cocktail diva Audrey Saunders developed this modern classic at the Bemelmans Bar (named for author and illustrator of the *Madeline* series of children's books) in New York's Carlyle Hotel. Earl Grey tea provides nuances of apricot and tart orange to an elegant libation crafted with Tanqueray Gin for its juniper-focused flavor and high proof.

3/4 ounce lemon juice, fresh
1 ounce simple syrup
1 1/2 ounce Earl Grey tea-infused dry gin*
1 egg white
lemon peel

Combine liquid ingredients in a mixing glass filled with cracked ice. Shake vigorously and strain into a chilled Martini glass. Express lemon peel over the glass, rub it around the rim, and drop it in.

*Measure 4 tablespoons loose, Earl Grey tea into 750-ml bottle of gin. Cap and shake, and let sit at room temperature for 2 hours. Strain through a fine sieve or coffee filter into a bowl. Rinse out bottle to remove loose tea, and pour infusion back into clean bottle.

64

BREAKFAST MARTINI

Once upon a time, cocktails were considered a morning drink – a bracer against the forthcoming day. Jams and marmalades appeared in cocktails, including one called the "Marmalade Cocktail," listed in *The Savoy Cocktail Book* of 1930. For his own modern, morning-inspired cocktail, London mixologist Salvatore Calabrese transforms customary Martini assembly, adding the orange expression of Cointreau and softening the backbone of gin, not with vermouth, but with marmalade. Serve with buttered toast on the side.

> 2 ounces dry gin
> 3/4 ounce Cointreau
> 3/4 ounce lemon juice, fresh
> 1 teaspoon orange marmalade
> orange peel

Combine liquid ingredients in a mixing glass filled with cracked ice. Shake vigorously and strain into a chilled coupe glass. Express orange peel over the glass, rub it around the rim, and drop it in.

PORNSTAR MARTINI

The first version of a Pornstar Martini, concocted by London mixologist Douglas Ankrah, is tweaked for the regulars at Vesper, a small boutique bar in Amsterdam with a focus on artisan cocktails. As for the recommended drinking ritual, start with a bite of the passion fruit, sip the cocktail, and finish with the side of fizzy Prosecco to clean the palate.

1 1/2 ounces vodka
1 ounce Monin Passionfruit Puree
1/2 ounce vanilla syrup*
1/2 passion fruit shell
Prosecco, chilled

Combine liquid ingredients in a mixing glass filled with cracked ice. Shake and strain into a chilled Martini glass. Float the passion fruit shell. Serve a shot of Prosecco on the side.

*Combine 1 cup sugar, 1 cup water, and 2 Madagascar vanilla beans in a small saucepan over medium heat and stir until sugar dissolves. Remove from heat and let cool to room temperature. Strain into a clean glass jar .

MARTINA

An elegant British brasserie and bar named in honor of the building's architect, The Gilbert Scott is located in the borough of St. Pancras, London. An evolving cocktail list, organized by mixologist Dav Eames includes an interpretation of the Martinez, early variant of the modern Martini, often described as a Manhattan made with Gin instead of Whiskey. Sweetness of Vermouth fills the first sip; the swallow offers gin with bursts of cardamom and coriander, intermixed with notes of ripe peach.

> 1 1/2 ounces dry gin
> 3/4 ounce Italian vermouth
> 1/2 ounce Bols Peach Liqueur
> 2 dashes Angostura Bitters
> orange peel

Combine liquid ingredients in a mixing glass filled with cracked ice. Stir briskly and strain into a chilled Martini glass. Express orange peel over the glass, rub it around the rim, and drop it in.

SUSAN SONTAG

Dedicated to the woman who wrote about the intersection of high and low art, this spirit-forward abstract work from Grandma's Bar in Sydney, Australia has the elegance of a Martini, with dramatic brushstrokes of mezcal, restrained floral hues, and undertones of ripe peach "brightened" with Peychaud's.

1 1/2 ounces mezcal
1 1/2 ounces French vermouth
1 dash Creme de Peache
2 dashes Peychaud's bitters
lemon peel

Combine liquid ingredients in a mixing glass filled with cracked ice. Stir briskly and strain into a chilled Martini glass. Express lemon peel over the glass, rub it around the rim, and drop it in.

BAMBI WARHOL

In Ian Fleming's *Casino Royale*, published in 1953, secret agent James Bond orders his Dry Martini with both gin and vodka, a drink later named the Vesper. At Artusi in Seattle, Washington, where Jason Stratton's passion for cocktails falls within the Italian palate, his dalliance with Mr. Bond's Martini anchors gin and vodka with an Italian aperitivo of fortified Moscato d'Asti steeped with bitters and citrus.

> 1 1/2 ounces dry gin
> 3/4 ounce vodka
> 1/4 ounce Cocchi Americano
> 1 dash orange bitters
> orange peel

Combine liquid ingredients in a mixing glass filled with cracked ice. Stir briskly and strain into a chilled Martini glass. Express orange peel over the glass, rub it around the rim, and drop it in.

BURNT MARTINI

In this rendering of the Martini, Scotch whisky stands in for vermouth, imparting a smoky note to the herbal character of the gin. The choice of the Scotch will, of course, determine savor and aroma. Single malts Laphroaig, Taliskar and Lagavulin provide the most smoke. Serve in a snifter to funnel the aroma of the Scotch toward your nose.

> 2 1/2 ounces dry gin
> 1 barspoon Scotch whisky
> lemon peel

Combine liquid ingredients in a mixing glass with cracked ice. Stir briskly and strain into a chilled snifter glass. Express lemon peel over the glass, rub it around the rim, and drop it in.

FRONTIER MEDICINE

Showman P. T. Barnum said "There's a sucker born every minute," prompting a post-Prohibition bartender to create a cocktail called Barnum was Right, a successful partnership of gin and brandy. At The Huguenot in New Paltz, New York, Derek Williams refines the herbal aspects of gin and fruity sweetness of Cognac for a lovely drink with a trifle of citrus tart for balance.

> 2 ounces dry gin
> 1 ounce Cognac
> 4 dashes orange bitters
> orange peel

Combine liquid ingredients in a mixing glass with cracked ice. Stir briskly and strain into a chilled snifter glass. Express orange peel over the glass, rub it around the rim, and drop it in.

BREAKFAST OF CHAMPIONS

Cocktails are often a mark of simultaneous frivolity and finesse. The Wheaties cereal slogan provides inspiration to Seth Sempere of Seattle's Spur Gastropub. And, like the waitress in Kurt Vonnegut's classic novel of the same name, bartender Bonnie MacMahon declares "Breakfast of Champions" each time she delivers the bitters-soaked Martini to a patron.

> 2 ounces dry gin
> 1 ounce French vermouth
> 2 ldashes orange bitters
> 2 ldashes grapefruit bitters
> 1 pinch of salt
> lemon peel
> grapefruit peel

Combine liquid ingredients in a mixing glass filled with cracked ice. Stir briskly and strain into a chilled Martini glass. Express lemon and grapefruit peels over the glass and drop them in.

DIANA ROSS

It resembles an inverted Martini, heavy on the aperitif and light on the Gin, inspired by "Upside Down," the 1980 disco song by Ms. Ross. "All the ingredients are kept chilled," explains mixologist Alam Rivas, who perfected the cocktail at the Canvas Club in Brisbane, Australia, "and it's shaken for 5 seconds rather than stirred, which makes the flavors more delicate and aromatic.

> 2 ounces Lillet Rosé
> 3/4 ounce dry gin
> 1/3 ounce Peche de Vigne
> grapefruit peel

Combine liquid ingredients in mixing glass filled with cracked ice. Shake and strain into a chilled Martini glass. Express grapefruit peel over the glass, rub it around the rim, and drop it in.

LA PERLE
DE MER

Perched on the 40th floor of the Heron Tower, Duck & Waffle is the highest restaurant in the UK. Looming over London, the establishment's bar program, developed by Richard Woods, has made its presence known to those below with eccentric, indulgent cocktails. Re-imagining the classic, Mr. Woods adds salty/savory notes to a Vodka Martini, infusing vermouth with oyster shells for a whisper of salinity and lovely mineral characters.

> 2 ounces vodka
> 1/2 ounce oyster-infused French vermouth*
> 1 raw oyster

Combine liquid ingredients in a mixing glass filled with cracked ice. Stir briskly and strain into a chilled Martini glass over the raw oyster.

*Add 8 oyster shells to a sealable container and cover with the contents of a 750-ml of vermouth. Leave to rest for 24 hours. Filter through a coffee filter and reserve until needed.

DOUBLE AGENT

"I'm the money," says Vesper Lynd, introducing herself to James Bond. "Every penny of it," he replies. Ian Fleming's cocktail, inspired by his character in 1953's *Casino Royale*, is revamped with the slightly sweet, deeply herbal flavors of Yellow Chartreuse in a drink that can be thought of as yet-another adaptation of the classic Martini.

> 2 ounces dry gin
> 1/4 ounce Yellow Chartrueuse
> 1/4 ounce Lillet Blanc

Combine ingredients in a mixing glass filled with cracked ice. Stir briskly and strain into a chilled Martini glass.

THE DUNHILL LIGHTER

Alfred Dunhill's first tobacconist and pipe shop opened in 1907 on Duke Street. Its proximity to the clubs of St. James's and Pall Mall ensured success, with a loyal and distinguished customer base. Dunhill has provided various accessories for the cinematic James Bond throughout the series. The association began in 1962 when the production team requested a gunmetal cigarette lighter for Sean Connery's introduction in *Dr. No*.

> 1 1 barspoon orange curacao
> 1 ounce dry gin
> 1 ounce dry sherry
> 1 ounce French vermouth
> 1 dash Pernod
> green olive

Combine liquid ingredients in a mixing glass filled with cracked ice. Stir briskly and strain into a chilled Martini glass. Drop olive into the glass.

FEMME FATALE

Chartreuse adds a seasoning of herbs and a brilliant green color that brightens the palate and transforms the classic Martini formula. You can make it dirty by adding a little olive juice if you like, or you can be a little more subtle and add the essence of olives by garnishing with three olives instead.

> 1 1/2 ounces dry gin
> 1/2 ounce Green Chartreuse
> 1/2 ounce French vermouth
> green olive

Combine liquid ingredients in a mixing glass filled with cracked ice. Stir briskly and strain into a chilled Martini glass. Drop olive into the glass.

PERPETUAL
SUNRISE

The mystical union of gin, Italian vermouth and Campari was conceived and popularized at the Caffé Casoni in Florence's famed Palazzo Strozzi, a hub of Anglo-Florentine sophistication during the interwar years. The traditionally simple, yet powerful recipe from Brooklyn's Nighthawk Cinema starts with a Chartreuse rinse and replaces Campari with a nip of Fernet-Branca. "Life is a great sunrise," wrote Nabokov.

> 1/2 ounce Green Chartreuse
> 1 1/2 ounces dry gin
> 1 ounce Italian vermouth
> 1/2 ounce Fernet-Branca

Fill a Martini glass with ice and let it sit until the glass is chilled. Once the glass is chilled, toss the ice, pour in Chartreuse, swirl it around to fully coat the interior walls of the glass, then discard. Combine gin, vermouth, and Fernert-Branca in a mixing glass filled with cracked ice. Stir briskly and strain into the prepared glass.

THE FITZGERALD

Nick Carraway enjoys a glass of Chartreuse on the night he first meets the elusive ant-hero in F. Scott Fitzgerald's *The Great Gatsby*: "Finally we came to Gatsby's own apartment, a bed-room and a bath, and an Adam study, where we sat down and drank a glass of some Chartreuse he took from a cupboard in the wall." In this homage to the great American novelist, a Martini framed with herbal complexity resonates with the theme of Gatsby's carefully cultivated world.

> 1 1/2 ounces dry gin
> 1/2 ounce French vermouth
> 1 barspoon Yellow Chartreuse
> 1 dash absinthe
> lemon peel

Combine liquid ingredients in a mixing glass filled with cracked ice. Stir briskly and strain into a chilled Martini glass. Express lemon peel over the glass, rub it around the rim, and drop it in.

MARTINI DI MILANO

A Fernet wash (or Fernet rinse) is the secret behind Milan's home-grown Martini cocktail, served at La Terrazza on Via Santa Radegonda. The method involves coating the inside of a glass with the amaro, discarding the excess liquid, then pouring the remaining ingredients into it. What provides the drink its distinction is the insistent presence of Fernet-Branca, whose big, burly personality in this case acts as a gentle nuance.

> 1/2 ounce Fernet-Branca
> 2 ounces dry gin
> 1 ounce Lillet
> 2 dashes Orange Bitters

Fill a Martini glass with ice and let it sit until the glass is chilled. Once the glass is chilled, toss the ice, pour in Fernet-Branca, swirl it around to fully coat the interior walls of the glass, then discard. Combine gin, Lillet, and bitters in a mixing glass filled with cracked ice. Stir briskly and strain into the prepared glass.

FITTY-FITTY

It is said the Martini spent the better part of the 1980s and '90s as a stripped-down version of itself. In an effort to reintroduce America to the joys of dry vermouth and orange bitters, Audrey Saunders created the sophisticated Fitty-Fitty cocktail at New York's Pegu Club. The modern "wet" Martini echoes the vintage Cornell cocktail.

> 1 1/2 ounces dry gin
> 1 1/2 ounces French vermouth
> 2 dashes orange bitters
> lemon peel

Combine liquid ingredients in a mixing glass filled with cracked ice. Stir briskly and strain into a chilled Martini glass. Express lemon peel over the glass, rub it around the rim, and drop it in.

GIN BLOSSOM

Is there a point at which the drink ceases to be a Martini? If it drifts too far off course, perhaps it should be called something else. Julie Reiner's (of Brooklyn's Clover Club) modern play on the Martini is an aromatic riff on the classic, mixing fruit notes of apricot with fragrant, floral notes of vermouth, and the herbaceous profile of gin.

> 1 1/2 ounces dry gin
> 1 1/2 ounces French vermouth
> 3/4 ounce apricot eau de vie
> 2 dashes orange bitters
> orange peel

Combine liquid ingredients in a mixing glass filled with cracked ice. Stir briskly and strain into a chilled Martini glass. Express orange peel over the glass, rub it around the rim, and drop it in.

SAKE-TINI

Sake, the national liquor of Japan, was first made at least 2,000 years ago. Since then, sake has played an important role in Japanese culture and history. Skilled Japanese bartenders partner the clear, rice-based liquor with vodka to create an homage to the American Martini. Cucumber, known for its cooling quality, gives this cocktail a mellow and refreshing flavor, while a twist of lime gives it a bit of energy.

    1 1/2 ounces sake
    1 1/2 ounces vodka
    1/8 ounce French vermouth
    cucumber ice cubes*
    lime peel

Combine liquid ingredients in a mixing glass filled with cucumber ice cubes. Shake vigorously and strain into a chilled Martini glass. Express lime peel over the glass, rub it around the rim, and drop it in.

*Peel and chop one cucumber and place it in a food processor or blender. Blitz well. Use a fine mesh strainer to extract the pulp, and pour the juice into an ice cube tray or desired mold. Freeze overnight.

HANAMI MARTINI

 Over the years, a uniquely Japanese style of bartending has evolved, with idiosyncratic methods for shaking drinks, preparing ice, and overall service. Barmen prepare the Hanami Martini with a cherry blossom, an enduring metaphor for the ephemeral nature of life. The word "hanami" refers to the centuries-old practice of picnicking under a blooming cherry blossom tree. The salted cherry blossom replaces the hint of saltiness of an olive.

> 2 1/2 ounces sake
> 1 ounce dry gin
> 1/4 teaspoon Maraschino liqueur
> salted cherry blossom

Combine liquid ingredients in a mixing glass filled with ice. Stir for 20 seconds. Strain into a chilled Martini glass and garnish with the salted cherry blossom.

WASABI MARTINI

London's most exclusive private club, Morton's has a stunning bar, running the length of the room, with large glass windows looking out onto the posh borough of Mayfair (which takes its name from the historic fortnight-long May Fair). The Wasabi Martini was invented at Morton's in 2004 by head bartender Philippe Guidi.

 2 ounces vodka
 1 pea-sized portion wasabi paste
 3/4 ounce lemon juice
 1/2 ounce simple syrup
 yaki-nori seaweed

Combine liquid ingredients in a mixing glass with cracked ice. Shake vigorously and strain into a chilled Martini glass. Garnish with seaweed.

ARNOLD PALMER MARTINI

He may not have been the first person to combine iced tea and lemonade, but when Arnold Palmer requested the drink after one hot day of golf in Palm Springs, a woman seated nearby thought that sounded refreshing and drew everyone's attention when she requested "an Arnold Palmer." The refreshing Martini lives up to its non-alcoholic namesake.

> 2 ounces tea-infused vodka*
> 1 1/2 ounces lemon juice, fresh
> 1 ounce simple syrup

Combine ingredients in a mixing glass with cracked ice. Shake vigorously and strain into a chilled Martini glass.

*Add 1/2 cup loose black tea to a 1-liter bottle of vodka, let sit overnight, then strain.

ROGER MOORE MARTINI

Replacing Sean Connery in the role of James Bond, Roger Moore played the consummate British secret agent in seven films across an eleven-year tenure – a debonair, more seasoned take on the character. Like all 007 agents, Moore's Bond drank his Vodka Martini shaken, not stirred. But, in a recipe he revealed in *Bond on Bond: Reflections on Fifty Years of James Bond Movies*, the real life Moore was a Martini purist, taking his drink murderously dry and cold.

> Noilly Prat Dry Vermouth
> Tanqueray Gin
> lemon peel

Fill 1/4 of a Martini glass with the vermouth. Swill it around and then discard it. Next, top the glasses up with gin, express lemon peel over the glass and drop it in. Place the glass in a freezer or ice-cold fridge until ready to serve.

BUNYAN

Named for the giant lumberjack in American folklore, the Bunyon is driest of all Martinis, yet one could say if you omit vermouth, you are not having a Martini at all. This drink contains no vermouth (or bitters), which puts your selection of gin at the center of attention. If you add orange bitters to the Bunyon, you'll have yourself a Jockey Club cocktail. Timberrr!

> 3 ounces dry gin
> 1 green olive

Add gin to a mixing glass filled with cracked ice. Stir briskly and strain into a chilled Martini glass. Drop olive into the glass.

A FEW PAGES FOR YOUR OWN RECIPES

Other Books by the Author:

Prosecco!
Italy's Iconic Sparkling Wine, with Cocktail Recipes and Lore

Bartender's Handshake
The Cult of Fernet-Branca, with Cocktail Recipes and Lore

Chartreuse
The Holy Grail of Mixology, with Cocktail Recipes and Lore

All the Gin Joints
New Spins on Gin from America's Best Bars

Out of Those Wet Clothes and Into a Dry Martini
A Charles Butterworth Witty Cocktail Guide

ReMixology
Classic Cocktails, Reconsidered and Reinvented

Cocktails at Dinner
Daring Pairings of Delicious Dishes and Enticing Mixed Drinks

63180736R00065